The Red Kites of Wales

Photo: Gerry Whitlow

INTRODUCTION

To the dedicated naturalist and casual onlooker alike there can be few sights in the British countryside to rival the spectacle of a Red Kite gliding low over a Welsh hillside. Just a few decades ago the possibility of such a chance encounter was as remote as the place in which it was likely to occur. A handful of breeding pairs, confined to their last refuge in the picturesque valleys of mid Wales, teetered on the brink of extinction for over half a century. Few people other than dedicated naturalists, keen birdwatchers and local farmers were privileged to observe their beauty, grace and aerial prowess. How quickly things can change!

The success story of the conservation of the Red Kite in Wales has been told many times in the media and still stands as one of the most successful conservation initiatives ever undertaken. Those associated with the Welsh Kite Trust today, in their many previous guises, played a major part in halting the decline of this magnificent bird. Foremost amongst these saviours of the Red Kite were three of our present Trustees, my co-author Peter Davis, Peter Walters Davies and John Davis, who, working for the Nature Conservancy and the Institute for Terrestrial Ecology, did much of the groundbreaking research on the Welsh Red Kite in its natural environment. Their fieldwork, along with later input from the RSPB's Research Department, identified the reasons for the very poor breeding success seen in Welsh kites during the 1970's & 80's. Acting on the information gained, conservation measures such as nest wardening, egg and chick manipulation and the supplementary feeding of chicks were all employed, with varying degrees of success, in an attempt to increase the number of young being produced.

Photo: Howard Nicholls

Helped by these endeavours, the 1993 Welsh Red Kite population exceeded one hundred breeding pairs for the first time in over a century and the delights of seeing this wonderful bird were now open to many more people over a much wider area. If every success story has to have a down side, ours was that this milestone event signalled a major cut in the level of funding available for kite protection and research. The formation of the Welsh Kite Trust in 1996 was an attempt to ensure that the kite's increase continued, allowing the opportunity for native birds to spread throughout Wales and to help re-colonise England through the Welsh Borders. In 2004 there was estimated to be nearly 500 pairs of Red Kites in Wales and the long awaited occupation of England began with a pair of kites rearing a single chick just over the border in Herefordshire.

Whilst we touch briefly on the great success story of kite conservation and give credit to the many people involved, this booklet's primary function is as an informative guide to the natural history of the Red Kite in Wales compiled from the extensive research carried out by the current staff and Trustees of the Welsh Kite Trust. Such extensive research is never a solo exercise. We owe a great deal to the Countryside Council for Wales (formerly Nature Conservancy Council) and the RSPB who in the past funded much of this work. Indeed CCW provided grant-aid towards the establishment of the Welsh Kite Trust, without which our formation may have floundered. The RSPB still maintains a small input through its reserve wardens and an annual contribution to the Trust towards our monitoring costs. The "Friends of the Welsh Kite" scheme is our primary source of funding and we thank anyone who supports us through this method. Finally we must also acknowledge the huge efforts made each year by our volunteer fieldworkers (the Welsh Kite Watchers' Group) who locate and monitor many of the nests. We are deeply indebted to them all for their continuing support.

The 'Swallow Buzzard'
Photo: Eithel Powell

PLUMAGE

In Wales one of the many local names for the Red Kite *Milvus milvus* is Boda Wennol or "Swallow Buzzard". This is a wonderfully descriptive name that exactly conjures up both the shape and grace of Wales' most famous breeding raptor. Considerably smaller than the two eagle species found in Britain and marginally smaller than the migratory Osprey, it is nonetheless an impressive bird close-up with a wing span of nearly two metres (about five and a half feet). In still air its flight can appear almost laboured, with deep slow wing-beats, and is very reminiscent of a Grey Heron.

A Red Kite easily evades the attentions of a jealous Carrion Crow. Photo: Mike Read

When soaring in thermals or riding the wind however it is easy to see why the child's toy was named after it. With a large wing area and relatively small body weight (around 900 - 1.300g or 2-3 pounds) the kite can remain in the air for many hours with scarcely a single beat of its wings but at the same time it has a turn of speed and a manoeuvrability which can amaze even experienced observers. These flying skills are best tested when trying to ward off the unwanted attentions of Carrion Crows or Ravens around the nest site or when avoiding the persistent dive bombing of an over-anxious Peregrine.

If all-round aerial expertise were not enough to inspire, the Red Kite also has good looks in its favour. With subtle blends of autumn colours the kite is surely one of the most beautiful of all raptors. In the adult the breast is a rich mahogany, streaked with black, whilst the feathers of the upperparts are a warm tawny brown, edged pale. The tail, at its best in full sunlight, is a rich orange with a deep fork and is surprisingly long (longer in relation to total body length than that of either the pheasant or the grey wagtail!). The head is pale grey, finely streaked with black, and the eyes, rather surprisingly, have broad white irises.

The sexes are not distinguishable on plumage but, in common with most other birds of prey, females average slightly larger than males. Juvenile kites are generally lighter in colour than the adults with a paler, sandy, breast with only faint dark streaking (see photos at left). The feathers of the upperparts (see photos on following pages) show

An adult (left) and a juvenile, showing the different head plumage. Photos: Gerry Whitlow & Mike Read (right)

The differences between the adult (above)and the juvenile are very evident in these two pictures. Photos: Iain H Leach

more contrast between the overall warm orange, the dark central streaks and the more extensive pale edging. The pale edging to the main wing coverts creates a thin whitish line running across the centre of the wings. The head is pale fawn coloured, with much less streaking and the iris, quite unlike that of the adult, is dull brown.

By far the commonest view obtained of a kite, however, is as it circles overhead. Here the long, forked, tail and long, angled, wings are the distinctive characteristics. On the underside of the wings there is an extensive white wing patch formed by the underside of the inner primaries and the bases of the outer primaries which contrasts strikingly with the black tips of the outer primaries and the dark, black-barred, secondary feathers. Red Kites, unlike Common Buzzards, are extremely uniform in the patterning of their plumage with one kite being quite indistinguishable from the next – unless, that is, it happens to be white! In Wales, one of the results of the genetic bottleneck which the population underwent earlier this century, is that occasionally chicks are born that lack the dark pigmentation in their feathers to varying degrees. The resultant birds range from a washed-out salmon pink version of the normal kite to almost complete albinos (see large picture on page 10). Unlike true albinos, however, the eyes are pale blue rather than pink and the cere and feet are yellow as normal. Several of these "white" kites have survived for a number of years after fledging but none have yet been found breeding.

An adult kite chases a juvenile, notice the duller tail and lighter wing patches of the juv. Photo: Howard Nicholls

In-flight studies of an adult (above) and a juvenile Red Kite. Note the pale edges to the wing coverts which form a distinct line in the middle of each wing of the juvenile. Photos: Iain H Leach

➤ *Although much paler the normal plumage pattern is still apparent. Photo: Iain H Leach*
➤ *A leucistic kite chick in the nest, this is the same bird as the large picture above. Photo: Tony Cross*
➤ *(Facing page) Another picture of the same bird showing just how white the plumage is once faded. Photo: Mike Attwood*

HISTORY OF THE RED KITE IN WALES

Until about 300 years ago, the Red Kite was breeding throughout the mainland of Great Britain and in some of the larger offshore islands, though apparently never in Ireland. The bird's decline in Britain was already in train by the early 18th century. Believed to be a frequent predator of young domestic fowls and gamebirds, this was among the least tolerated birds of prey, and one of the easiest to exterminate by gun, trap, poison, and the destruction of nests. Improvements in small firearms, and the development of game preservation on the estates of the landed gentry, together with environmental changes such as woodland clearance and agricultural enclosures of waste land, tipped the balance against the kite. By 1800 the population was in steep decline, and the bird was probably already extinct in several English counties (Buckingham, Cheshire, Middlesex) and in nearly all of southern Scotland, and greatly reduced and fragmented elsewhere.

The process accelerated into the 19th century, with added threats posed by a new vogue for taxidermy and egg-collecting. By the 1840's there were breeding kites in no more than 15 of the 39 English shire counties, and probably none in Scotland south of the Forth-Clyde divide. In the 1860's kites bred in only four English counties, Gloucestershire, Hampshire, Lincolnshire, and Shropshire, all in districts with extensive areas of woodland. Only in Shropshire did they apparently survive past 1870, but a few years later they had gone. In Scotland after 1860 kites were confined to some seven Highland counties, and after 1880 they probably bred in only three, Inverness, Ross and Cromarty, and Caithness. The last breeding occurred in the mid- 1880's, and the Red Kite was extinct in Scotland by the early 1890's.

In Wales the same forces were at work, though they were eventually to be moderated. There are no early records from Anglesey and west Carnarvonshire, nor from south and west Pembrokeshire, and it may be that kites were never common in the exposed western extremities of the country. They had probably gone from Flintshire and much of Denbigh (as from neighbouring Cheshire) before 1800, but lingered on in the Conwy valley until perhaps 1830, and in Montgomery and Merioneth until the 1850's. In the south, they seem to have been extinguished in Pembrokeshire and Glamorgan about the same decade. In Monmouthshire they perhaps survived as late as 1870. By the 1880's breeding kites were confined to north Carmarthenshire, north-east Cardiganshire, north Breconshire, and south-east and west Radnorshire.

In Britain as a whole, ornithologists were very slow to appreciate the rapidity and extent of the slide towards extinction. Since most of them were collectors, many were perhaps concerned to obtain specimens before the supply was exhausted; or unwilling to admit their contribution to the decline. Eminent writers were still speculating about the status of the kite in parts of England and in Scotland, twenty years after the last kites had died. In Wales we were fortunate, in that several locally-based naturalists came to know the real situation, before it was too late to take action.

PROTECTION AND CONSERVATION IN WALES

The first to act was Edward Cambridge Phillips, Justices' Clerk in Brecon, and author of the first Birds of Breconshire (1882). Connected by profession and by marriage to the local squirearchy, Phillips was able to influence landowners in north Breconshire to discourage the destruction of kites on their estates. He noted with some satisfaction the increasing numbers of kites in the upper Usk and Honddu valleys during the 1880's, to perhaps a dozen pairs. These efforts at protection were recognised by a special vote of thanks, passed by the council of the Zoological Society of London in 1890. Sadly, the employment of several Scots gamekeepers on certain estates resulted in a battue of the Usk valley kites, and no fewer than 8 or 9 were known to have been killed in 1889, five of

One of the last native Red Kites in Britain, near the RSPB Dinas reserve in the early 1900's. Photo: H. Morrey Salmon

them on a single estate near Brecon. Within twenty years, the last of the Usk kites had gone. A similar slaughter by keepers on estates in the Wye valley below Builth removed that population by the early 1900's. One keeper in 1902 claimed to have killed 30 kites in as many years. Meanwhile in north-west Breconshire and west Radnorshire a protection scheme had been started around 1890 by Phillips's brother-in-law Alfred Gwynne Vaughan, a Builth Wells solicitor, and Vaughan's friend the Rev. David Edmondes Owen, Rector of nearby Llanelwedd. They combined to pay rewards to farming tenants with nesting kites, and were the first to place barbed wire on trees, in an attempt to discourage nest robberies. Unfortunately their efforts were not sufficient to counter the commercial demand for eggs and young birds. Each specimen could command the equivalent of a month's wages for local men. Very few recorded nests were left unmolested in the 1890's and early 1900's.

Dr. John H. Salter came to teach botany at Aberystwyth in 1891, and it is through his diaries that we learn most about the Welsh kites at the turn of the century. Salter was an experienced all-round naturalist and also a man of great vigour and presence. He ranged widely through central Wales, interviewing local people, following any lead, and meticulously recording all he could learn. He met Gwynne Vaughan and Edmondes Owen, later visited Cambridge Phillips, and in the new century collaborated with the Sussex ornithologist and collector J. Walpole Bond, who had settled in 1902 near Builth, where he wrote *Bird Life in Wild Wales*.

THE KITE.

THE FORK-TAILED KITE, AND GLEAD.

Milvus vulgaris.

Already in 1898 Salter was writing in he *Zoologist* magazine about the great threat to the survival of the Kite, posed particularly by egg collectors. In 1900 the senior British bird society, the British Ornithologists Club, passed a resolution stating that any member found destroying kites "should be visited with the severest censure". On 13 February 1903, Salter wrote to the BOC, proposing the establishment of a protection scheme. He was supported by F. C. R. Jourdain. On 18 February the BOC agreed to set up a Kite Committee, and to devote substantial funds to the payment of local watchers at selected nest sites. Salter was asked to make the local arrangements, but since he was based at some distance, he seems to have delegated much of the task to Vaughan and Owen among others, though he remained responsible for the payments to watchers. Bond's part in the scheme was highly ambiguous. He claimed to be an active participant, yet it is clear from his diaries that he knew each year of several nests which he did not divulge to the BOC or its local representatives. Bond continued to visit the kite area annually until at least 1908, which was also the year when Salter departed to live abroad.

From 1905 the main BOC contact became E.G.B.Meade-Waldo, who visited the area annually to receive the reports of the watchers. He was to retain overall responsibility for kite protection until the early 1930's, wearing his BOC hat until 1922, and later acting for the RSPB. Vaughan and Owen played a vital role locally. Owen moved to become Vicar of Llandovery in 1911, and he recruited the help of Col. Dudley Williams Drummond, Land Agent to Lord Cawdor, the principal landowner in the Upper Tywi valley. Drummond took over the administration of the watchers in that district for several years from 1913. Alfred Gwynne Vaughan died in 1915.

Possibly the first photo of a Welsh Red Kite at the nest. Photo: Arthur Brook

It should be emphasised that at no time did the protection scheme embrace the whole kite population. Outlying pairs, often unknown to the BOC, and only very intermittently recorded for posterity, were left to fend for themselves. It is very probable, however, that in the early years of protection the Welsh Kite population continued to contract. Around 20 pairs are recorded for the 1890's, 15 or so for the early 1900's, but for a year or two around 1910 there may have been no more than 10 or 12 pairs, confined to the upper Tywi and Cothi valleys in Carmarthenshire and the upper catchment of the Wye in Breconshire. Improved breeding success by the protected pairs, and the publicity attached to kite protection, then allowed the population to stabilise or even to increase a little, aided by a lull in persecution during the First World War.

The immediate post-war period in 1919-22 seems to have been disastrous. Edmondes Owen reported that unruly discharged soldiers were known to have shot several kites in 1920-21, and that extensive felling of woodland was causing much disturbance. Breeding success collapsed. In 1922, six or seven known nests produced only two fledged young altogether. Edmondes Owen himself died suddenly in August. Later that year, the BOC passed over responsibility for kite protection to the RSPB Watchers Committee, chaired by Meade-Waldo.

A new local representative was needed, and Meade-Waldo chose the Rev. W. J. Constable, a retired public school master living near Llandovery. Constable took a very limited view of his responsibilities, and confined his interest to the upper Tywi valley. He relied mainly upon one local keeper for assistance in 1923, but fortunately a retired police inspector, A. W. Jones, offered his services in 1924. He ran the watching scheme with great efficiency until 1939. Meanwhile Salter had returned to live near Aberystwyth in 1923, and became involved again with the kites. Meade-Waldo provided him with details of the known breeding records since 1903. Salter garnered other records from his own sources, and began to visit outlying areas, mostly with negative results, though he located a previously unrecorded pair in the Crychan Forest north of Llandovery, and was informed of another at Ffarmers. Constable' s obsession with secrecy extended even to Salter, and their relationship remained formal, though Salter soon established a rapport with Inspector Jones.

During the 1920's the kite population showed no sign of increasing from a level of perhaps 10-12 pairs (6 or 7 under protection), and may even have declined. Productivity in most years was discouragingly low. A number of unfortunate events received publicity. The policeman at Cilycwm attempted to sell an egg to a visitor in 1926; he was reprimanded and removed elsewhere. The

Red Kite eggs proved an irresistible lure even to some of the early nest watchers. Photo: Tony Cross

Cardiff ornithologist H. Morrey Salmon photographed a nest near Rhandirmwyn in 1928, and was reproved by Mrs. Lemon, the RSPB Watchers Committee's formidable secretary. He thereupon resigned from the Society. Then in 1930 Desmond Nethersole-Thompson robbed a nest near Cynghordy, exhibited the eggs at a British Oologists Association meeting in 1931, and wrote an account of his exploit in *The Field* in 1932. Several prominent members of the BOA resigned in protest, and an acrimonious correspondence in *The Oologists' Record, The Field,* and elsewhere rumbled on until 1935.

A very early flight shot, a considerable achievment with the photographic equipment of the day. Photo: W. M. Condry

Widespread discontent with the RSPB' s protection scheme, and internal intrigues in the Society's senior committees, mainly directed against Mrs. Lemon, now flared into open criticism. H. F. Witherby, President of the British Ornithologists Union, proposed in 1932 the creation of a 'British Kite Trust', to try to save the kite; 36 BOU members offered to become trustees, but the idea was allowed to lapse. In March 1933 E. M.Nicholson and Morrey Salmon attacked the RSPB's performance in the *Daily Mail*. The Society responded by announcing a 'new approach' to kite protection in November 1933. A special leaflet was circulated as part of a 'wide public appeal' to landowners, farmers, keepers, and 'people in authority' to do everything in their power to protect the kite. Lord Forester had now become Chairman of the Watchers Committee in succession to Meade-Waldo, who died early in 1934. Towards the end of 1934 the Society agreed to employ Miss Dorothy Raikes of Bwlch, Brecon, who had been nominated by Mrs. Lemon's critics, to search for kites in outlying areas. She travelled fairly widely in 1935- 37 , but did not produce any additional pairs.

The period 1931-35 was probably the nadir of the Red Kite population in Wales. Although up to 11 pairs are known to have existed, some did not attempt to breed, and only two are thought to have reared young. In some years, only a single chick fledged. This was probably the time of the genetic bottleneck in the population, discovered by research nearly 60 years later. Henceforward there was only one remaining female line of descent, from the old British stock.

Matters hardly improved during 1936-40, though an outlying pair bred near Tregaron in 1939. Constable finally resigned in autumn 1937. He proposed Guy Lloyd of Cynghordy as his successor, but Dorothy Raikes was appointed instead. It had been another bad year for the protectionists, since one of the watchers was detected offering a clutch of eggs for sale, and despite efforts to conceal the affair, it soon became public knowledge. A prosecution proved impracticable, since it was only an offence to take the eggs, not to possess them, and proof of the theft was lacking. Mrs Lemon resigned from her position in 1939, following her 'defeat' by the pro-Raikes faction. She had served the RSPB continuously since 1891. Miss Raikes, while accepting an annual sum from the Society towards expenses, launched a very successful independent fund-raising campaign in Wales in 1938, and went her own way, providing the RSPB with only the briefest of annual reports. The nest-watcher scheme virtually ended in 1939, though the payment of rewards to farmers and others continued.

A 1906 photograph of three Welsh chicks in the nest. Photo: C. Kearton

The limited amount of fieldwork done during the Second World War was carried out mainly by the eminent botanist Mrs Irene M. Vaughan of Rhandirmwyn, with the help of a local schoolmaster, B. F. Thomas; though Dorothy Raikes was able to visit the Tywi valley at times. Both Salter and Constable died in 1942. In 1945, exasperated by the lack of detailed reports, the RSPB Council asked James Fisher to visit Dorothy Raikes and drive her round the kite country. He later reported favourably on her 'system', and said that all the British kites could be visited on one day! Miss Raikes was ill in 1946 and Mrs Vaughan took over as supervisor. Fisher visited again, always with a retinue, in 1946 and 1947, and produced several articles and radio broadcasts about the kites. Miss Raikes ceased to be directly involved after the 1948 season, due to incapacity.

Capt. H. R. H. Vaughan had retired from the Navy, rejoined his wife at Rhandirmwyn, and taken up her interest in the Kite. He was not a field naturalist, but a natural organiser. In 1949 he approached the West Wales Field Society with the suggestion that it should take over the organisation of kite protection. In October the WWFS set up a 'Kite Preservation Sub-Committee', with Capt. Vaughan as chairman and Mrs Vaughan as secretary, with representatives of the WWFS and the RSPB among the membership. At a further meeting in January 1950 this was replaced by an ad hoc Kite Committee embracing representatives of several relevant societies, the funds to be administered by WWFS. Miss Raikes did not attend, though she eventually made over her residual funds in 1953. The RSPB continued to provide money for bounty payments. Morrey Salmon was appointed to act as Kite Recorder, and started to amass kite data for his celebrated long-term record.

There were in practice two separate 'Kite Committees' from the start, the *ad hoc* formal one, which met only irregularly and at long intervals, and the informal gathering of voluntary watchers and others, who met at least annually to discuss fieldwork and the outcome of each season. The formal committee was soon embroiled in controversy, containing as it did several strong and opinionated individuals, notably Capt. Vaughan and R. M. Lockley of the WWFS. There were disagreements about the use of confidential information, about research proposals (especially ringing), and particularly about the administration of the Kite Fund. Finally in 1956 Vaughan resigned as chairman, and the formal committee effectively ceased to function.

Matters were not finally resolved until March 1958, at a meeting in Carmarthen with Lord Hurcomb (Nature Conservancy) in the

➢ *An adult kite in flight, showing its superb tail to best advantage. Photo: Iain H Leach*

chair. Here it was agreed to dissolve the formal Kite Committee, the balance of its funds to be handed to the RSPB, which would accept responsibility for future 'special measures' and bounty payments. The Nature Conservancy undertook to carry out ecological research on the kite. Capt. Vaughan' s informal committee continued to run local kite monitoring until 1970, with the co-operation from 1960 onwards of professional wardens from the Nature Conservancy and the RSPB.

The respite from persecution given by the Second World War allowed the kite to increase to around a dozen breeding pairs by 1950. The

The Kite Committee in 1964: (back row left to right) R. S. Thomas, Peter Panting, Tommy Warren Davis, R. H Baillie, William Condry, Capt. Vaughan, Dr. Clifford Fenn. (front row) Penny Condry, H. Morrey Salmon & Mrs. Vaughan.

breeding range was extended northwards into Cardiganshire, and a few birds had returned to the upper Wye. Capt. Vaughan's active team of voluntary watchers, including Mrs. Vaughan, William Condry, Dr. Clifford Fenn, R. H. Baillie, and later the poet R. S. Thomas, besides a wide circle of other contacts, was able to monitor the population more effectively than ever before. They were joined in 1960 by Peter Panting for the Nature Conservancy at Tregaron, followed by Peter Davis in 1966, and by a succession of RSPB wardens at Rhandirmwyn. Kite numbers rose slowly and erratically until the mid-1980's, but then more rapidly as new pairs occupied more productive lowland sites and became more successful at rearing young. We now know also that a wild female from the continent must have joined the Welsh colony in the 1970's, introducing new blood.

There were many obstacles and setbacks to recovery along the way. These included a recrudescence of egg collecting, the advent of myxomatosis in 1955 (rabbits were a favoured prey), and the impact of two consecutive severe winters in 1962-63; but also generally poor nest productivity, related to an erratic food supply and a wet climate, and perhaps complicated by pesticide pollution; and to genetic problems ('in- breeding'). Last but not least, there was excessive mortality of full-grown birds, from the widespread use of poison baits set for crows and foxes.

Media interest and changing public attitudes have led to a reduction in the level of poisoning.

Public attitudes towards the kite were gradually changing, bringing increasing sympathy for protection and conservation, and a growing attachment to the bird as a symbol of Welsh individuality. This was perhaps reflected in the growing involvement of public and voluntary bodies in the fieldwork. The Nature Conservancy and the RSPB, with the full agreement of the Vaughan committee, and the continuing participation of volunteers in the annual survey, took over the reins in 1970. They put increasing resources into monitoring, protection, and research during the 1970's and 1980's, fought against an apparently co-ordinated onslaught by the egg-collecting fraternity (up to 25% of all nests were robbed in some years), campaigned for a reduction in poisoning, and helped the Kite to eventually win through.

CURRENT POPULATION AND DISTRIBUTION

The Red Kite has a very limited geographical range which, with the exception of the small and isolated populations in N W Africa and West Transcaucasia, is entirely confined to Europe. The total world population was recently estimated at only 19,000 - 23,000 breeding pairs with the main centres of population occurring in Germany (c.13,000 breeding pairs), Spain (c.4,500 breeding pairs) and France (c.2,800 breeding pairs). At the time of the first co-ordinated UK survey in 2000, Great Britain held approximately 450 breeding pairs, with at least 250 of these in Wales. Unlike the core populations in Germany, Spain and France (which are all experiencing declines due to habitat change, persecution and secondary poisoning) the Welsh population is growing rapidly. By 2004, it alone was almost certainly in excess of 450 breeding pairs and it is possible that in excess of 1,000 young Red Kites fledged in Britain as a whole during 2004!

MAP SHOWING CURRENT WELSH RANGE AND CORE AREA Figure 1

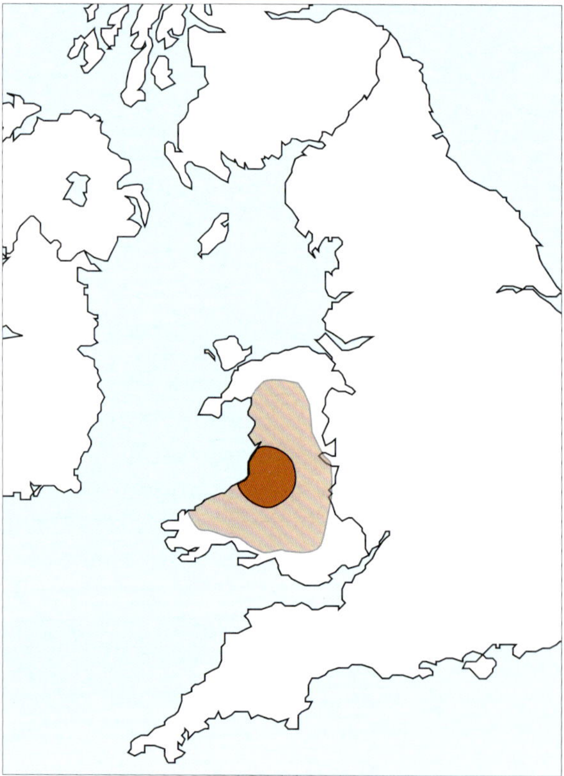

It is always difficult to strike a balance between the need to inform an ever-increasing public interest in natural history and a reluctance to make widely available, information which some may use for illegal and destructive purposes. This has always been an acute problem as far as the Red Kite is concerned due to the threat of nest robberies by egg-collectors. Because of this, we make no apologies for the necessarily vague map shown in Figure 1. The lighter brown area encompasses the whole known breeding range of the Red Kite in Wales, up to and including 2004, but includes some areas where the kite does not yet breed. The darker centre marks the core area where the majority of pairs can be found and which is already well known to both birdwatchers and egg-thieves alike. This map is changing all the time. In 1986 the central dark area would have served equally well to display almost the entire breeding range of the Red Kite in Britain, for it is only since this date that the population in Wales has shown any signs of a substantial increase (see Figure 2 below).

WELSH RED KITE POPULATIONS 1969 - 2004 Figure 2

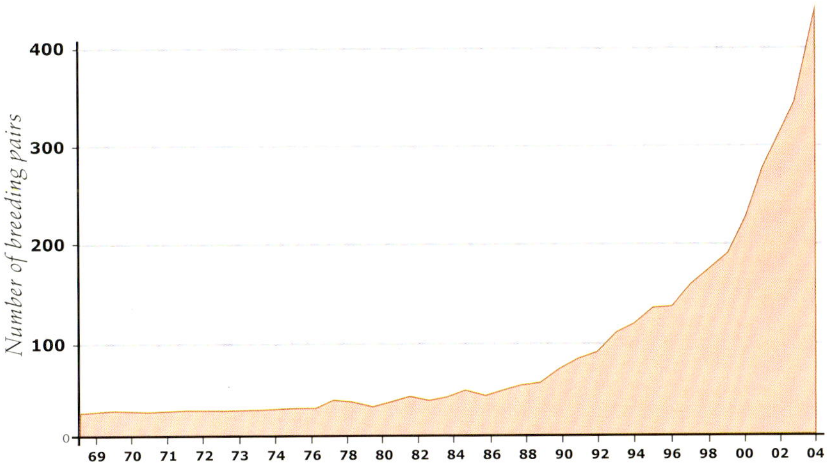

RED KITE RE-INTRODUCTIONS

In the mid 1980's, The Joint Nature Conservation Committee (JNCC) and RSPB held discussions on the practicalities of re-introducing Red Kites to their former range in England and Scotland. At this time the Welsh population stood at about 40 pairs, had low productivity and was thought to be isolated and vulnerable. It showed absolutely no sign of the increases to follow. Clearly it could not withstand the harvesting of enough chicks to furnish these plans so moves were made to secure sources in Spain, Sweden and Germany. Releases commenced in 1989 under a partnership arrangement between English Nature and RSPB in the Chilterns in England, and RSPB and Scottish Natural Heritage on the Black Isle in Scotland. A small number of Welsh bred chicks were given over to these re-introduction projects but only where it was not possible to relocate them into suitable foster nests within

Wales. These projects met with overwhelming success, so much so that subsequent releases in the East Midlands, Stirling, Yorkshire, Dumfries and Galloway largely used the progeny of the very successful initial releases, particularly those in the Chilterns.

During 2004, a fourth English release scheme, the last planned official release, was started near Gateshead in Tyne and Weir (the first such urban fringe release scheme). Odd pairs of kites are now starting to spring up in many English and Scottish counties where they haven't nested for well over one hundred years including Wiltshire, Hampshire, Sussex, Devon, Cambridgeshire, Berkshire and Rutland. Birds of presumed Welsh origin nested successfully in Herefordshire in 2004 and Shropshire too may well have had its first breeding kites since it became the last English county to lose its native kites in the 1870's, although confirmation is lacking. In addition to these deliberate introductions, in the last few years of the century, a pair presumed to be of continental origin (both adults were untagged), started to breed in Suffolk. This pair managed to rear at least eight young in three years before disappearing. Figure 3 shows the location of the official release schemes with the first year of release.

MAP SHOWING LOCATION OF OFFICIAL RELEASE SCHEMES Figure 3

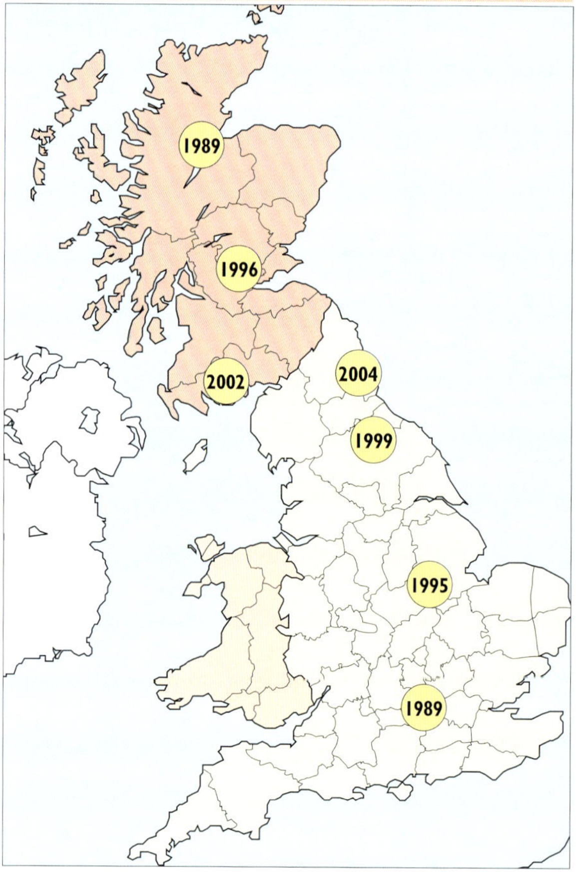

Historically the Red Kite occurred throughout most of Britain in large numbers and with proper protection measures and continuing support there is no reason why they should not do so again in the future.

HABITAT PREFERENCES AND FOOD

Kites are essentially birds that range widely from woodland areas, where they roost and breed, to scavenge and hunt over areas of open country. In Wales they tend to be associated with the rolling hills of the Cambrian Mountains with their grass moors and low intensity pastoral farming system. Here kites are able to exploit the high numbers of small mammals (mainly voles and young rabbits) but also take a large number of small to medium sized birds, especially young Carrion Crows, Rooks and Magpies. Other live prey such as frogs, lizards and beetles are also eaten and earthworms form a fairly substantial part of the diet, especially in the spring. Particularly during the winter, kites are also fairly reliant on sheep carrion and, to a lesser extent, human refuse. They will readily take advantage of butcher's off-cuts put out specifically for them at "kite feeding stations" ** . The association with the uplands, however, is a fairly artificial one and arises as a result of the persecution in the 18th and 19th centuries, which confined them to the hills as a `last refuge'. Recently kites have started to re-occupy the more fertile lowland areas with their largely improved pastures. These areas are a more ready source of earthworms and crow and rabbit populations tend to be higher there. It is these factors that have given rise to increased productivity in recent years.

On the continent the Red Kite inhabits a range of similar open habitats from temperate woodlands to arid savanna-type terrain. In a few places they can still be found scavenging around towns and villages, although not as regularly as their close relative the Black Kite. This habit was formerly common in Britain and there are many references to kites helping to keep the streets of London clean in the Middle Ages. This useful service was appreciated to such an extent that the Red Kite and the Raven were the first birds to be given royal protection in Britain.

*** Kite feeding stations now need to be licensed by DEFRA. Any food put out needs to comply with current regulations on the disposal of meat by-products. See Appendix.*

COURTSHIP AND NEST-BUILDING

Except for those at the highest altitudes, adult kites in Wales tend to remain at or near their breeding territories all winter, perhaps making local movements out of the hills after heavy snowfalls or during periods of prolonged freezing. The onset of the breeding season is therefore a fairly gradual process. On fine days as early as late January pairs may be seen circling over their nest-woods or carrying the odd stick to a previous year's nest. In the mid 1990's a pair was recorded building a fairly substantial nest during late September and mid October but needless to say lost interest as the weather turned colder. For established pairs courtship and nest-building usually start in earnest during March, about 2-4 weeks before the first egg is laid, but first time breeders may not start until April. Courtship in the Red Kite is on the whole a fairly simple affair. Both members of the pair soar together over the nest-wood often to great heights. They will also indulge in mild flight-play with one bird approaching the other then parting again. Either singly or as a pair the birds will occasionally spiral steeply out of the sky and swoop up to the nest. Kites are more vocal than usual at this time of the year and the pair will often call to one another with a shrill whinnying. Copulations are frequent and serve to reinforce the pair bond.

Kites occasionally lock talons. Photo: Gerry Whitlow

The spectacular chasing around the sky and infrequent "talon-grappling" and "falling leaf" behaviour which are also observed in spring are often aggressive encounters between rivals but may sometimes occur during courtship.

In Wales, nests are built exclusively in trees, with a strong preference for hardwoods, especially oak, and beech. The nest itself is a fairly flat and untidy structure of sticks, approximately 60cm (2ft) across and placed in a substantial fork or often balanced on a horizontal branch away from the main trunk. They are built at a height of 4-30 metres (12-100ft) above the ground with the majority being between 12-15 metres (40-50ft). Nest-building starts fairly gradually with both members of the pair bringing sticks to the nest. The sticks are usually collected from the ground but are occasionally snapped off nearby trees. Sticks are usually carried to the nest in the bill and both sexes build the nest. The previous year`s nest, if available, is often re-used, especially if the birds were successful in rearing young. At other times the pair may build a new nest from scratch or refurbish an old nest of Carrion Crow, Raven or Buzzard. Most nest-building activity takes place during the late mornings or occasionally in the evening. Kites are notoriously sensitive to disturbance at this stage and will readily move site if disturbed**.

An adult at the nest. Photo: Howard Nicholls

This stage of nest building can take as little as a few days to as long as a few weeks. As egg laying approaches, both birds start to collect pieces of wool or fur, dry grass, moss and the occasional piece of rag, paper or plastic with which to line the nest. The nest cup is shallow and approximately 30 cm (1ft) in diameter.

***The Red Kite is listed under Schedule 1 of the Wildlife and Countryside Act 1981. This means that from the initial stages of nest-building to the time when the young become independent of the adults the nest-site is protected by special penalties. Under the Countryside and Rights of Way Act 2000 anyone found recklessly disturbing an active nest, attempting to steal eggs or harming adults or dependent young could find themselves facing a substantial fine or possibly even 6 months imprisonment. Licences are required to visit nests for monitoring, ringing young or photography.*

AGE OF FIRST BREEDING

Welsh Red Kites usually breed for the first time when they are 2 or 3 years old although some birds do not breed until they are older.

The following information (Figure 4) is based on a sample of 555 wing-tagged young kites that fledged successfully during the years 1975-1993. Up to and including the 2000 breeding season, a total of 187 have subsequently been found breeding - 94 males, 87 females and 6 unsexed.

AGE OF FIRST BREEDING IN WELSH KITES Figure 4

1st	**summer**	**No birds bred but 5 individuals are known to have paired**	
2nd	**summer**	**45 males, 34 females, 2 unsexed bred**	**= 81 birds (43.5%)**
3rd	**summer**	**28 males, 28 females, 3 unsexed bred**	**= 59 birds (31.5%)**
4th	**summer**	**11 males, 12 females, 1 unsexed bred**	**= 24 birds (13%)**
5th	**summer**	**5 males, 5 females bred**	**= 10 birds (5.5%)**
>5th	**summer**	**3 males, 4 females bred**	**= 7 birds (3.5%)**

6 others (2 males and 4 females) bred at unknown age (3%).

92 males first bred at an average age of 2.86 years and 83 females at an average age of 2.98 years.

There are only five records of 1st year Welsh tagged juveniles apparently paired up and settling at a nest-site. In all five cases the pairs dispersed early on without reaching the egg laying stage. Re-introduced birds in both Scotland and England have been reported to have nested and successfully reared young in their first summer although the occurrence is infrequent. One particularly precocious released kite actually became a grandfather at 2 years old!

Red Kites generally pair for life, although this is probably more through a mutual attachment to the same territory and nest sites rather than any great attachment to each other. There are a few recorded cases of divorces where both members of the original pair were later found breeding with different partners.

EGGS

The eggs of the Red Kite, so sought after by egg collectors that they will risk heavy fines (up to £5,000/egg) or even six months imprisonment to obtain them, are actually rather unimpressive. Although a few eggs are well marked most are largely white with just a few brownish red blotches or lines. The eggs are slightly larger than an average chicken egg, approximately 57 x 45 mm with a slightly matt surface. The photograph below shows a collection of kite eggs, all taken from nests in Wales. This selfish activity was a major factor in the length of time it took the population to re-establish itself and start expanding again.

CLUTCH SIZE AND INCUBATION

The eggs are usually laid in the last week of March or the first two weeks of April, although late clutches by first time breeders may be laid as late as early May. Eggs are normally laid at three-day intervals. The timing of the first egg is somewhat dependent on the weather with clutches being laid slightly later in cold and wet springs. Kites in Wales lay between one and four eggs with two or three being by far the most usual number (see Figure 5). Only one clutch per year is laid but a small percentage of pairs will relay if their first clutch is lost or stolen early in the incubation period.

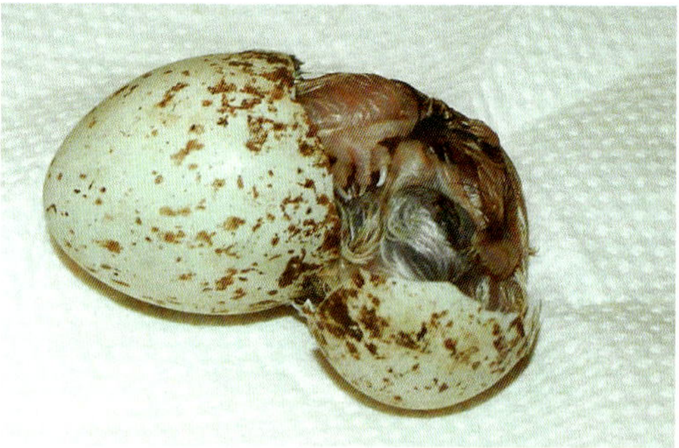

CLUTCH SIZES IN WELSH KITE NESTS Figure 5

	No. Clutches	Percentage
1 Egg	**51**	**6.8**
2 Eggs	**399**	**53.5**
3 Eggs	**281**	**37.7**
4 Eggs	**15**	**2.0**
	Data for 746 clutch sizes in Wales during 1946 – 1996	

Incubation is carried out largely by the female, fed on the nest by the male, and starts with the first egg. Males will incubate for short periods, usually less than 30 minutes, whilst the females go off to feed, hunt or preen. Eggs are occasionally left uncovered for short periods but the parents remain within sight of the nest. During cold and wet weather females may stay on the nest continuously for considerable periods. At one nest being monitored by remote video camera the female remained nearly motionless on the nest for over 36 hrs during a period of prolonged high winds and heavy rain. Other birds have been observed sitting under a covering of snow. Incubation lasts for approximately 32 days per egg (31-35 days) with the chicks hatching at about two or three day intervals.

Kite chicks hatch with a thick covering of pale sandy brown down, slightly darker on the back. The down on the top of the head is long and spiky giving them a distinctly punk-like appearance. Soon after hatching the young are fed by the female with small pieces of meat torn off whatever has been brought to the nest by the male. This pattern is maintained for about the first two/three weeks until the young are able to tear at the food themselves. Kite chicks hatch at two to three day intervals so the young in the nest are of differing sizes. Sibling aggression is common and the larger chick will peck vigorously at its younger nest-mates if they attempt to get food before it has had its fill. Younger chicks respond to this beating by lying prone in the nest with their head down. The female will instinctively feed the largest chick because it is nearest to her and begging the most. Once the largest chick has finished the others will get what is left. If enough food is available all the chicks should survive. In nests where food is in short supply the size difference between the chicks will increase with the smaller one(s) ultimately either dying of starvation or being killed by the larger chick(s). This is a harsh but perfectly normal situation and ensures that at least one of them gets sufficient food. In Welsh kites a single chick reared is by far the commonest outcome. Broods of two chicks though are not infrequent and some pairs even manage three (see figure 6). Although less frequent, multiple chick nests actually account for a greater percentage of all young fledged. This demonstrates how high quality adults, producing multiple chick broods, can make a relatively greater input into future generations than those rearing just a single chick.

A five day old chick with its recently hatched sibling.
Photo: Tony Cross

The frequency of broods of three chicks is increasing in Welsh Red Kites, however the commonest brood size is still a single chick as below.
Photos: Tony Cross

Red Kite chicks instinctively lie down flat and still, when disturbed at the nest.
Photo: Tony Cross

FLEDGED BROOD SIZES IN WELSH KITE NESTS Figure 6

	1946-1994			1995 - 1999			2000 - 2004		
	No. of broods	% of broods	% of chicks	No. of broods	% of broods	% of chicks	No. of broods	% of broods	% of chicks
Brood 1	489	65	47.4	306	62.8	44.6	365	62.4	43.8
Brood 2	245	32.6	47.4	163	33.5	47.5	192	32.8	46.1
Brood 3	18	2.4	5.2	18	3.7	7.9	28	4.8	10.9
n =	752			487			585		

Data for 1824 fledged brood sizes in Wales 1946 - 2004

PRODUCTIVITY IN WELSH KITE NESTS 1951 - 99 Figure 7

Period	Number of Breeding Attempts	Number of Young Fledged	Number of Young /breeding pair	Number of Young /successful pair	Breeding Success Rate
1951-60	104	79	0.76	1.32	57.69%
1961-70	180	102	0.57	1.38	41.11%
1971-80	287	189	0.66	1.42	46.34%
1981-90	442	348	0.79	1.40	56.11%
1991-99	1132	1043	0.92	1.43	64.49%

The data above (figures 6 & 7) show how the productivity of Welsh kite nests has improved slightly in recent years. As well as more nests being successful there are slightly more chicks per successful nest. Even though the proportion of broods of three young has nearly doubled, there is not a single recorded instance of a pair of kites in Wales rearing four chicks to fledging although this is not uncommon on the continent and has already happened in both the English and the Scottish re-introduced populations. The relatively low productivity of Welsh kites is thought to be partly due to genetic factors, partly due to the adverse weather conditions and partly because of a combination of low prey abundance and a high level of inter-specific competition for food with Common Buzzards and Ravens.

After about 3 or 4 weeks the female starts to leave the chicks alone at the nest whilst she goes off to help the male provision the young. Sibling aggression has usually started to fall off by this age and any remaining chicks are likely to survive, although the smaller chicks may take much longer to fledge than the older ones. During these later stages the adults just drop food off at the nest and the chicks feed themselves. The young make their first flight at about 7 - 8 weeks old but normally remain in the immediate vicinity of the nest for a further 2 or 3 weeks and they are still fed by the adults.

CAUSES OF NEST FAILURE

Because of the conservation attention given to Red Kites during the breeding season there is a great deal of information on the reasons why a large number of nesting attempts fail. Data collected during the period 1946 to 1996 shows there were 736 recorded instances of total nest failure in breeding kites in Wales out of a total of 1655 known nesting attempts (see Fig. 8). In approximately two thirds of all cases a reason for the nest failure was evident. The commonest recorded cause of nest failure was a completely infertile clutch. The level of infertility in Welsh kites during the period was very high and was almost certainly related to genetic problems associated with inbreeding. The second commonest cause was the deliberate stealing of kite eggs by illegal collectors. In several years in the 1980's almost a quarter of all known nests were robbed, usually as a result of the persistent activities of a very small number of individuals. Other causes of failure were the predation of eggs by crows or ravens, intentional and unintentional human disturbance, nests falling down or being blown out of the tree, the death of an adult or poor parenting by inexperienced breeders. In the remaining one third of all cases, where a reason for failure was not evident, around half failed on or around the expected hatch date.

CAUSES OF NEST FAILURE 1946 -1996 (n=736) Figure. 8

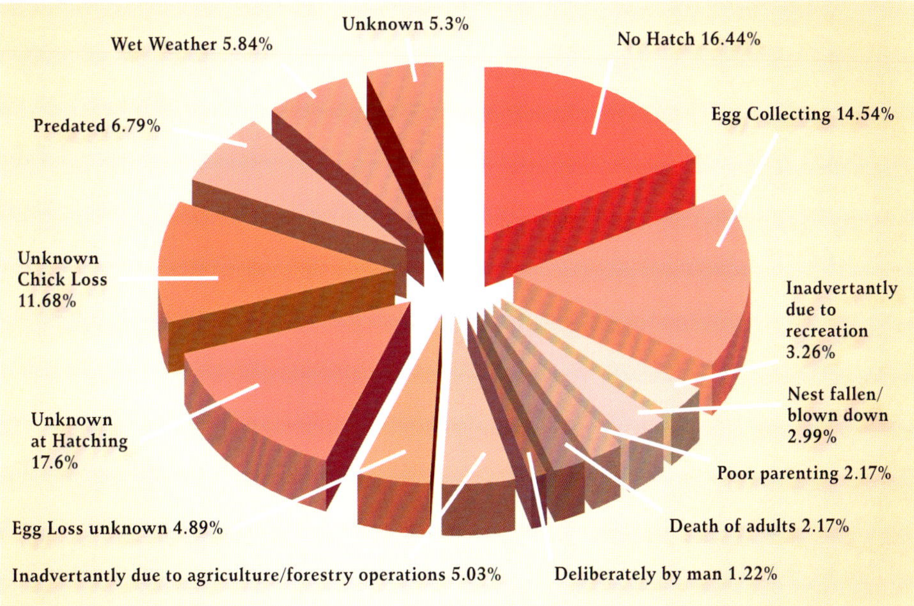

The weather, especially wet and cold weather, is thought likely to have played a significant part in many of the nest failures around hatching time; but this was difficult to prove.

In more recent years the relative importance of these causes of failure have changed. Infertility rates have declined, as has the level of illegal egg-collecting. Generally, although still low compared to many of the re-introduced populations, kites enjoy increased breeding success and moderately greater productivity. Poor weather and inadvertent human disturbance are now the major causes of nest failure identified.

MOULT

Bird feathers are relatively delicate structures which the bird relies on totally in order to fly. The keratin in feathers however is bleached by sunlight and the constant rubbing against branches and other feathers wears away the edges. Feathers may also get broken in fights or pursuits or whilst flying through trees. A lost feather is quickly replaced at any time of the year but a worn or broken feather, with the quill still in the follicle is not. To ensure that feathers are kept in good condition most birds replace their feathers on an annual basis, a process called a moult.

Feathers abrade at the tips. Photo: Tony Cross

Moulting is usually done in the summer when there are long days, good weather and ample food supplies. In some birds such as geese, ducks and swans the flight feathers are all moulted at once and the birds become temporarily flightless. Kites, in common with most other birds, need to retain their powers of flight so they undergo a gradual sequential replacement of the main flight feathers. Juvenile kites, hatched the

Note the symmetrical gaps in the wings. Photo: Mike Attwood

previous year, go into moult first, usually starting in late April. These are followed by failed breeding birds. Successful breeding birds delay their moult until later in the season when young are near fledging as they need to be in good flying condition to provision these chicks. The main flight feathers are shed from the centre of the wing towards the wingtip and create noticeable gaps in the wing (see photograph above). The tail feathers are moulted at the same time usually starting with the central two and the outside two giving it a very uneven appearance. Kites in the middle of a moult look incredibly tatty and indeed must find flight more difficult as they seem to spend much more time just sitting around.

In June, July and August, with practise, the stage of moult of a kite can be an obvious indication of its breeding status. A bird close to completion of moult is likely to be a non-breeder or failed breeder, a tatty bird very heavily in moult is a breeding bird rapidly replacing its feathers after the rigours of rearing young. Birds with a neat wing outline and scarcely a feather out of place are the current years young not long out of the nest.

MOVEMENTS

In Wales the kite is essentially sedentary, although some young birds disperse widely from their natal areas in the first year or two after fledging. During the period 1968-2004 nearly 2000 Welsh-bred young kites have been fitted with British Trust for Ornithology metal leg rings inscribed with a unique identification number. In addition, 1000 of these birds have also been fitted with plastic wing-tags which allowed individual identification at a distance. To date only 25 positive sightings or ring recoveries have been received of these birds outside of mainland Wales (see Figure 9). A notable feature of these exceptionally long movements is that they are normally undertaken by young birds within a few weeks of leaving the nest. Two examples illustrate this point. A juvenile which fledged the nest on an unusually early date in late June 1992 was found perched on a North Sea gas rig off the N. Norfolk coast (390 km from its nest) on 19th July. Similarly a 1970 chick, which fledged at a more usual date in early July, was found dead (over the body of a parrot!) on a railway line in Kent (315km from its nest) on 13th August. Most young kites, however, seldom travel more than about 40km from their birth place. The only confirmed overseas crossing so far obtained for a Welsh reared kite is of a 1995 chick from the heart of the kite's range near Llandovery

MOVEMENTS OF WELSH KITES OUT OF WALES Figure 9

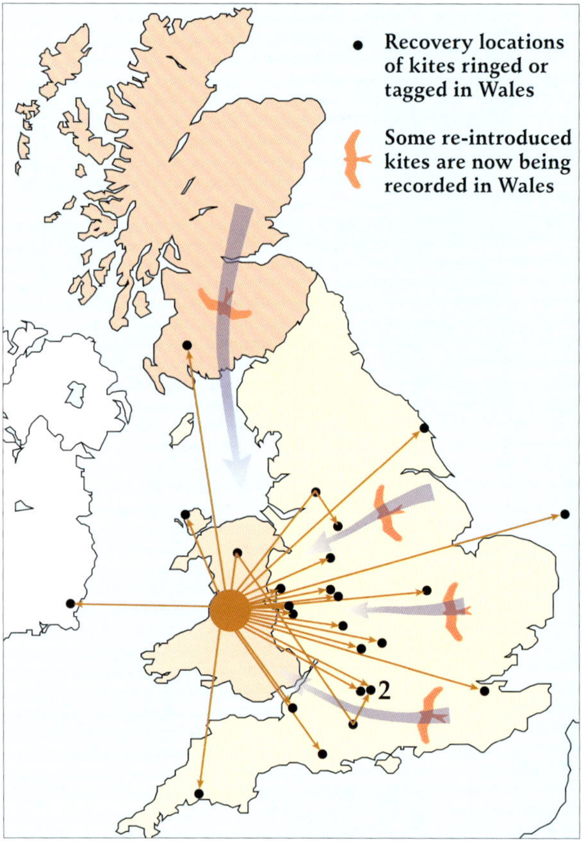

found dead at Ballyvaldon, Blackwater, County Wexford, Ireland on 20th October 1999.

Data collected up to 2000 on 144 individually identified Welsh kites marked as chicks and subsequently found nesting shows most bred very near to where they were reared. Males averaged 11.7 km from their birthplace to their first nest with females averaging slightly further at 13.7km. This strong attachment to their natal area explains why kites have been slow at reclaiming their previous range. Expansion tends to occur by new pairs settling on the periphery of the existing range rather than making spectacular leaps across unoccupied territory.

In north and central Europe kites are largely migratory, although there is an increasing tendency for some birds to over-winter nearer home. Swedish and German birds have a predominantly south-westerly bias in these movements with France, Spain, Portugal and N. Africa being the main destination for the winter period. Occasionally continental birds reach Britain. For example, a chick ringed in Schleswig-Holstein (West Germany) was found near Rhayader in July of the following year and another from Sachsen (East Germany) was found in Essex in April. Autumn migrations usually start in August with birds reaching the Iberian wintering quarters in late September. Return migration starts in late February reaching northernmost breeding grounds by late March or April. Spanish birds, like those in Wales, are fairly sedentary. Not surprisingly, reintroduced kites largely retain the migratory instincts of the population from which they originated. Scottish reared young - which were largely derived from birds of Swedish or East German origin - exhibit the greatest tendency to make occasional long distance movements south during the autumn. In May 1999 a 1998 born chick from Ross-shire was found dead as a result of a collision with powerlines at Viscaya near Bilbao, Spain and a 2003 Stirling chick was found injured near Airao in Portugal the following winter. A much more extraordinary movement is that of a 1997 Inverness-shire reared chick which turned up on the coastal plains of southern Iceland during December of its first year!

CAUSES OF DEATH AND LIFE EXPECTANCY

Because kites are relatively large and because of their great rarity a relatively high proportion of dead kites are found and subsequently reported or handed in. Any kite found freshly dead is automatically

CAUSES OF DEATH OF FULL-GROWN KITES IN WALES Fig. 10

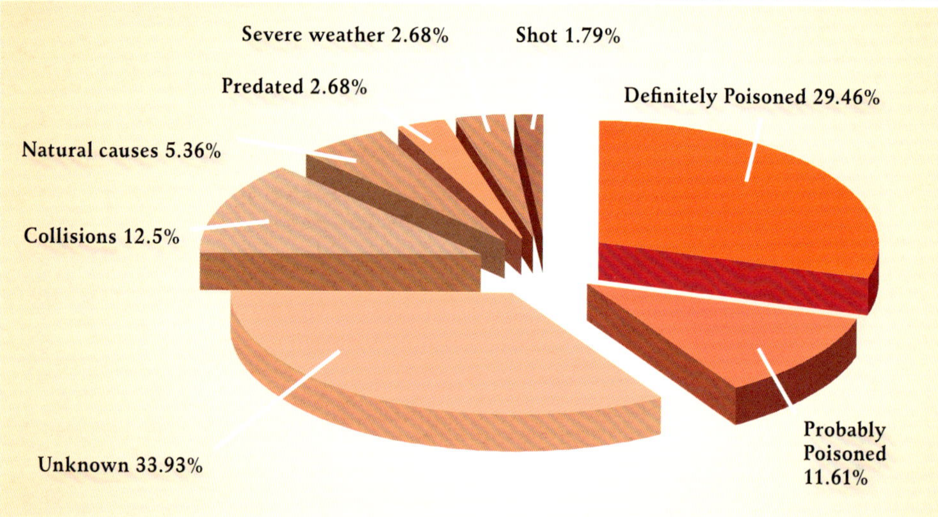

submitted to a Veterinary Investigation Centre (VIC) so that the cause of death can be ascertained. Data has been collected on 155 full-grown Welsh Red Kites found dead between 1950 and 1999. For 99 of these birds a cause of death was determined whilst for 56 the cause of death was quite unknown (see Fig 10). The results make distressing reading. Even taking all 56 deaths where the cause was unknown to be natural deaths (which they undoubtedly were not), a half of all kites died at the hands of man. In total 38 had definitely died due to poisoning and another 18 had probably died due to poisoning, 18 had died due to collision with wires, vehicles or aircraft and 3 had been shot. Clearly the illegal use of poisoned baits, none of which would have been set

specifically for kites, was a major problem. Most poison baits are laid in spring, during the lambing period, in order to control foxes and crows. It is not surprising therefore that this was the period of greatest mortality for Welsh kites at that time. Stiffening of the law on poison baits - which makes landowners more responsible for baits set on their land whether they set them or not, a major publicity campaign by RSPB and MAFF, and tougher fines have already gone a long way towards lessening the impact of this illegal activity. These measures were one of a combination of factors that allowed for the recent and dramatic population increases of kites in Wales. Recent submissions of kite carcasses to VIC's have shown a dramatic reduction in the number of cases of poison abuse with fewer cases now than when the kite population was merely a tenth of its current size. Secondary poisoning by new powerful rodenticides is now seen as a greater threat to kites.

< *Photo: Tony Cross* ∨ *Photo: Mike Attwood*

During the period 1968 to 1990 422 ringed young red kites fledged from the nest in Wales. Up to the end of 2000 a total of 70 of these birds had been found dead and the rings returned. Based on this information about one third of all Welsh Red Kites die in their first year. In subsequent years there is an 81% survival from one year to the next with at least 41% of all chicks fledged living to the mean age of first breeding at 3 years old. The oldest ringed wild kite so far recorded was a German bird that lived to be 26. In Wales the oldest recorded was almost 24 years old when it died and there have been several others approaching the 20-year old mark.

WING TAGS EXPLAINED

Much of the information on Red Kite movements and survival rates presented in this booklet was derived from long-term studies of wing-tagged individuals. Wing-tagging, although admittedly a bit unsightly, is a very valuable marking method that has been shown to be completely safe for the birds. Two thin, flexible, PVC tags are fitted to chicks in the nest, one to each wing. Following an agreed national coding system all kites tagged in Wales have a black tag on the left wing. The right tag colour represents the year of fledging and is consistent throughout all regional schemes. The table below, shows the tag colours used each year from 2002 – 2006 (tagging was resumed in Wales in 2002 after an eight year break). Each tag bears a bar of the opposite tag colour at the base so that a bird can still be identified even if only one tag is visible. With the aid of binoculars or a telescope fieldworkers can collect multiple sightings of an individual kite throughout its lifetime without ever having to trap or handle it again.

This kite shows two clearly visible tags. Photo: M D Hayward

2003

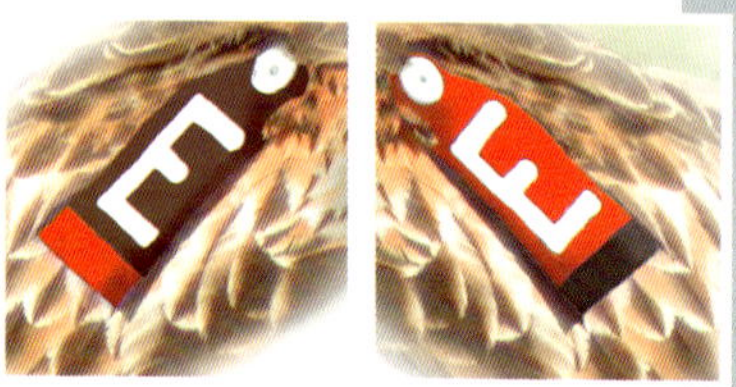

2002	**=**	**White**
2003	**=**	**Red**
2004	**=**	**Yellow**
2005	**=**	**Orange**
2006	**=**	**Green**

ACKNOWLEDGEMENTS

We are particularly indebted to the photographers who, without exception have provided their images free of charge - this booklet would not look anywhere near as good without their superb images.

Thanks are due to the Countryside Council for Wales and its predecessors; ITE; and RSPB for funding much of the work in the past, to all the past and present members of the Welsh Kite Watchers' Group (and its forerunners) and to all those too numerous to mention who have participated in voluntary kite wardening. Thanks are also due to all the land-owners who have helped to protect nests and allowed us access for research and monitoring. Finally without the continued support of the many subscribing *"Friends of the Welsh Kite"* it would be impossible to continue our work in Wales.

Tony Cross and Peter Davis

Photo: Mike Attwood

An early illustration of a Red Kite.

GUIDELINES FOR FEEDING RED KITES

An increasing number of individuals in different parts of Wales are feeding Red Kites, either for personal interest or as a commercial venture. At present, as long as the EU Animal By-Products Regulation is adhered to, it is perfectly legal to set up a feeding station at any time of the year. However, in order to prevent problems from occurring the Welsh Kite Trust strongly recommends that would-be feeders follow the guidelines set out below.

WHEN PROVIDING FOOD FOR RED KITES AT FEEDING STATIONS, IT IS RECOMMENDED THAT:

All neighbouring landowners and other local people are fully aware of the proposed activity and they are not strongly opposed. The feeding will almost certainly attract the attentions of rooks, crows, ravens and possibly large gulls. Disgruntled neighbours could present a threat to the Red Kites and other birds.

Feeding is carried out in the afternoon. This allows birds time to forage and hunt normally during the morning. Food provided at the feeding station would then constitute a top-up for those birds that had not been able to find enough to eat rather than a staple winter diet.

Feeding is done regularly at the same time every day. This would be particularly important in periods of cold weather, with deep snow or hard frost, and also during periods of very wet and windy weather. The kites may rely on the food being there rather than going elsewhere to look for it.

OTHER CONSIDERATIONS TO BE BORNE IN MIND:

All feeding activities must meet current Animal By-product Regulations. Before setting up a feeding station check with your local Environmental Health Officer and County Trading Standards Officer that they have no objection to the proposals.

In general, any meat fit for human consumption may be used but best check with the officers mentioned above for a ruling before commencing. Specified Risk Material or whole ruminant carcases must not be used.

Remove any remaining meat by the end of the day it is put out, in order to prevent wild mammals from eating it.

There should be no possibility of livestock gaining access to the meat, so that there is no risk of disease transfer.In most cases, the fat content of the meat being used (often likely to be butcher's off-cuts) will be very high. This is not a particular cause of concern but, if feeding is carried out in the summer, the fat content should be very much lower, as it will be less suitable for growing chicks in the nest. The amount of meat put out in spring and summer should be decreased so that it is just enough to maintain the kites' presence. The meat should be unprocessed and should have no additives (including salt). The use of meat, and especially poultry, from an intensively reared source, where it is likely to have received large doses of hormones and/or antibiotics, should be avoided.

Calcium deficiency may be a problem in birds receiving a large part of their diet from meat that does not contain bones. It may be that calcium supplements should be added to the food put out, but a better alternative is to ensure that some whole carcases of game, or day-old chicks, are included, to ensure that some fur and bone is provided. This will also be of benefit in enabling the birds to form pellets for regurgitation.

If feeding whole carcasses of game (deer, rabbits, pheasants etc), use animals shot with rifles rather than shotguns, as ingested lead pellets could cause lead poisoning.

Become a 'Friend of the Welsh Kite'

The Welsh Kite Trust runs a *'Friends of the Welsh Kite'* scheme. On joining "Friends" receive a copy of this booklet, an enamelled metal badge and a car-sticker. They also receive the latest editions of our twice yearly newsletter *'Boda Wennol'*, which includes updates on the status of the re-introduced populations in England and Scotland. If you do not wish to receive a further copy of this booklet you can tick the appropriate box and claim a £2.50 discount on your first years subscription.

Most important of all, income from Friends of the Welsh Kite enables us to continue our important work.

To save cutting your book, a form is available by post or as a download from our website

YES, I want to support the conservation of the Red Kites of Wales. Please enrol me as a 'Friend of the Welsh Kite'

I enclose my annual subscription of:

I/we do not wish to receive another copy of the booklet and have deducted £2.50 from my/our subscription fee ☐

Individual sponsor	**£ 10**	☐	**Group Sponsors**	**£50**	☐
Family/Joint Sponsor	**£ 15**	☐	**Corporate Sponsors min**	**£200**	☐

I would also like to enclose a donation of: **£ 10** ☐ **£20** ☐ **£50** ☐ **Other** ☐

I enclose my cheque to The Welsh Kite Trust, for: **£** ☐

NAME :
Mr Mrs Miss Ms

ADDRESS :

POSTCODE :

Gift Aid **I am a UK tax payer and would like the Welsh Kite Trust to treat my subscription/donation, together with any future payments as Gift Aid for the purpose of reclaiming tax.**

Signed . . . .